Egrets and Hippos

By Kevin Cunningham

21st Century
Junior Library

Published in the United States of America by
Cherry Lake Publishing
Ann Arbor, Michigan
www.cherrylakepublishing.com

Content Adviser: Stephen Ditchkoff, Professor of Wildlife Ecology and Management, Auburn University, Alabama
Reading Adviser: Marla Conn MS, Ed., Literacy specialist, Read-Ability, Inc.

Photo Credits: © PB_Images/istock, cover, 1, 4; © corlaffra/Shutterstock, 6; © Bwana Mkuba/Shutterstock, 8;
© Neale Cousland/Shutterstock, 10; © Maggy Meyer/Shutterstock, 12; © Stephan Ratts/Shutterstock, 14;
© Naturfoto-Online / Alamy Stock Photo, 16; © Serge Vero/Shutterstock, 18; © Craig Lovell / Eagle Visions Photography / Alamy
Stock Photo, 20

Library of Congress Cataloging-in-Publication Data

Names: Cunningham, Kevin, 1966- author.
Title: Egrets and hippos / Kevin Cunningham.
Description: Ann Arbor, MI : Cherry Lake Publishing, [2016] | Series: Better together |
    Audience: K to grade 3.
Identifiers: LCCN 2015049537| ISBN 9781634710817 (hardcover) | ISBN 9781634712798 (pbk.) |
    ISBN 9781634711807 (pdf) | ISBN 9781634713788 (ebook)
Subjects: LCSH: Mutualism (Biology)—Juvenile literature. | Cattle egret—Juvenile literature. |
    Hippopotamus—Juvenile literature. | Animal behavior—Juvenile literature.
Classification: LCC QH548.3 .C86 2016 | DDC 591.7/85—dc23
LC record available at http://lccn.loc.gov/2015049537

Cherry Lake Publishing would like to acknowledge the work of The Partnership for 21st Century Skills.
Please visit *www.p21.org* for more information.

Printed in the United States of America
Corporate Graphics

CONTENTS

The word *hippopotamus* means "river horse."

Teaming Up

A gray hippopotamus moves from the water to the shore. The hippo walks through high grass to its favorite feeding place.

A white bird swoops down. The cattle egret lands on the hippo's back. It knows the hippo will not hurt it.

Cattle egrets and hippos work together. Their **partnership** goes both ways. Each helps the other survive.

African elephants are the largest land animals in the world.

Cattle egrets are from Africa and Asia. They also live in the United States.

Cattle egrets learned a trick in Africa. The trick helped them form partnerships. The bird landed on an elephant. The elephant didn't mind. Many large **mammals** let cattle egrets land on them. The birds stood on cattle. They stood on rhinos. They also stood on hippos. It was like standing on a safe island.

Look!

Hippos and elephants have a lot in common. They also have a lot of differences. How many similarities and differences between the hippo and elephant can you think of?

Hippos are Africa's most dangerous animal.
They kill more humans each year than lions do.

Mighty Hippos

A hippo wants other animals to stay back. It will charge at any creature that gets close. Hippos even sink boats.

An angry hippo is scary. It stands between 11 and 16.5 feet (3.4 and 5 meters) long. Males weigh from 3,500 to 9,000 pounds (1,587 to 4,082 kilograms). Hippos crush bones with their huge teeth. On land, they can outrun the

Predators are plentiful in the African savanna.

fastest humans. People living near hippos know to keep away.

A hippo leaves the water as the sun goes down. It likes to eat on land during the cool evening. A group of hippos marches through the tall grass. Hippos eat plants at a certain place every night.

Predators hide in the grass. Predators hunt other animals for food. Hippos are neighbors with predators like lions and hyenas. Not even a lion will attack an adult hippo. But predators may try to grab a hippo **calf**. A hippo calf cannot fight

Humans weigh about 7.5 pounds (3.4 kg) when born.
Newborn hippos can be up to 13 times heavier!

predators. It only weighs 75 to 100 pounds (34 to 45 kg) when born.

The cattle egret helps protect the hippos. How? It turns out the bird makes a great **lookout**.

Ask Questions!

What objects around you weigh more than a hippo? Ask a teacher, parent, or librarian to help you find out. Is a refrigerator heavier? How about a car? How about a fire truck?

Hippos can be dangerous, but egrets know they are not a threat.

Keeping Watch

The cattle egret can land on a hippo's back with no problem. The bird sees a long way from up there. It can spot predators.

Cattle egrets must keep a lookout at all times. Predators might eat them, too. The sight of a lion or crocodile makes a cattle egret nervous. It makes a *kok-kok* sound to warn other cattle egrets.

A pod of hippos can easily protect its young with enough warning.

Hippos also know the *kok-kok* call means danger. A hippo **pod** bunches up when it hears the sound. A male leads a hippo pod. It lives with 10 to 20 adult females. That many hippos will scare even the hungriest predator.

The cattle egret gains an **advantage**, too. The hippos in the pod stir up insects as they march. Cattle egrets get an easy meal. They also get a ride. Standing on the hippo helps the birds save energy.

The cattle egret settles down in the brush for the night. Its stomach is full. The hippos finish eating. They return to

Hippos and egrets are very different, but they help one another survive on the savanna.

the water. Both animals dodged predators another day. The partnership between the hippo and cattle egret has worked again.

Think!

Think of the ways you look around to learn things. What does the weather tell you? Why do you stop at crosswalks to see? The cattle egret uses the back of a hippo as a lookout spot. Where could you go to be a lookout?

GLOSSARY

advantage (ad-VAN-tij) something that helps a creature

calf (KAF) a baby hippo

diet (DYE-it) the foods an animal eats

lookout (LOOK-owt) a creature that keeps watch

mammals (MAM-uhlz) animals with hair that nurse their babies with milk

partnership (PAHRT-nur-ship) two or more creatures that team up

pod (PAHD) a group of hippos

predators (PRED-uh-turz) animals that hunt other animals for food

FIND OUT MORE

BOOKS

London, Jonathan, with Matthew Trueman. *Hippos Are Huge!*
Somerville, MA: Candlewick, 2015.

Reyes, Gabrielle. *Odd Animal Helpers*. New York: Scholastic, 2011.

Shea, Therese M. *20 Fun Facts About Hippos*. New York: Gareth
Stevens, 2012.

WEB SITES

African Wildlife Foundation—Hippopotamus
www.awf.org/wildlife-conservation/hippopotamus

Saint Louis Zoo—Cattle Egret
www.stlzoo.org/animals/abouttheanimals/birds
/heronsflamingosibisspoonbi/cattleegret

YouTube—Animal Partnerships
www.youtube.com/watch?v=Qqa0OPbdvjw

INDEX

ABOUT THE AUTHOR

Kevin Cunningham is the author of more than 60 books. He lives near Chicago.